For Gary,

Who opened the doors that turned
the idea for this book in to a reality.

Thank you.

Rosa (rose) Dianthus (carnation or pink) and Alstroemeria.

Flowers & Imagination

Gillian & Alan Wheeler

stichting kunstboek

> "I must have flowers, always, and always."
> *Claude Monet*

I was introduced to Alan Wheeler back in the 1970s by my mother, Iris Webb, who was President of the National Association of Flower Arrangement Societies (NAFAS), RHS Gold medallist and author of a classic book on the subject: The Complete Guide to Flower & Foliage Arrangement.

She had the highest regard for Alan's professional skills and talents, enjoyed his wicked sense of humour and, apart from working together, they formed a deep and long-lasting friendship which continued the rest of my mother's life. Through Alan I then met Gillian, whose charm and creativity perfectly complemented Alan's, and everyone agreed that it was an ideal match when they married and an added blessing when Ross and Fleur were born.

Alan and Gillian's combined talents have now come together to create this very special book. The title alone speaks of Gillian's amazing skill with flowers and Alan's brilliant imagination. Alan was kind enough to design our Country Diary of an Edwardian Lady boutique, to show off the merchandise inspired by the book, soon after we published this international bestseller.

Having now published nearly 400 other books I know how much work and detail has to go into the text, photography, design and production of an illustrated book. This superbly produced volume reflects the passion for flowers and design that is the authors' hallmark. It also demonstrates their very high standards.

You, the reader, are in for a special treat as you are about to open this jewel box of colour and style and every page will give you some valuable inspiration. You will be sharing the secrets of style and creativity that have made Gillian and Alan so successful and I know that you will enjoy learning from their exceptional skills. My mother would have certainly been very proud of their achievement both with this book and also with the unique Covent Garden Academy of Flowers.

Richard Webb, Dartmouth
April 2013

Introduction

Gillian and Alan have been married for some time and although they have worked together on a wide range of projects both of them suddenly realised that they had not considered a book together. Gillian is the Principal and Founder of The Covent Garden Academy of Flowers. Their daughter, Fleur, is the buyer and creative stylist for The Academy shop. Fleur has an instinctive eye for style and colour and plays a valuable part in the whole enterprise. When the title Flowers and Imagination was suggested there was an immediate positive response. The two key words: 'Flowers' and 'Imagination' sum up the essence of Gillian and Alan's work. The title then became the trigger for what followed. The images, ideas and words in this book were created to reflect their passion for the dramatic, the decorative and the inventive.

Both Gillian and Alan have a wealth of experience in a number of creative areas: display, graphic design, decoration, exhibition and styling. They have often worked together lecturing or exhibiting their art work, paintings and collages both in London and beyond. Although they share similar views and agree on many projects, their ideas and skills are varied and complimentary. Gillian has always been passionate about flowers, foliage and living plant materials; she never tires of the endless textures, colours and forms that are all from nature. Alan, on the other hand, after many years of handling display materials and merchandise, adores the different forms one can create from paper and textiles. Putting the two together is second nature to Alan, and styling all manner of materials together with flowers still excites him. Gillian and Alan's passions work well together and apart, and they both have a very critical approach to their finished pieces.

This book is intended to help inspire, surprise and suggest a new direction or combination of colours, and to juxtapose two or three items that take the eye by surprise. The unexpected always gives a buzz to the onlooker, as does the gentle romance of more traditional themes. Whether they are creating the simplest or the grandest of displays, both Gillian and Alan love what they do. Come on their journey with them and enjoy. Flowers themselves are always a pleasure and when combined with an imaginative method of presentation they really take flight. The joy that flowers bring Gillian and Alan is endless and they both still very much enjoy inspiring amateurs and professionals alike at their Academy in Covent Garden.

'Flowers and Imagination'

Let me start by talking about the two key words in the title of the book. First, the 'Flowers', as without them the pictures and The Academy itself would not exist. Flowers are around us all of our lives in one form or another – so much so that we can take them for granted. They almost become a visual cliché. I want you to consider flowers from a slightly different perspective, without being too pretentious – to see them as an art form; to look upon their colours and textures as an artist looks at paint; to see their structure and form as a sculptor views their clay or stone. Once you can grasp the idea of Tulips, Roses or indeed any other flowers or foliage waiting in their buckets of water to be transformed, you are well on your way to becoming a flower designer.

All of this does not mean torturing your plant material into unnatural shapes. I firmly believe that simple treatments and classic lines are among the most attractive forms of flower decoration. The flowers we have to hand, however, can form exquisite pieces by exploring the wealth of textures, colours and shapes we have to work with.

I still get that buzz of excitement when creating new projects and schemes. I know Alan has exactly the same feeling of discovery when creating a new collage or paper sculpture. This is a constant factor in both our endeavours as designers, and I think it is a necessary ingredient if you want to explore and invent with flowers.

Throughout history, flowers in their natural state (wild or cultivated) have taken their place in everyday life. One only has to visit Kew Gardens or The British Museum to witness what the great botanists and artists of past centuries have given us. The flower as a symbol or an illuminated manuscript runs like a thread throughout history. We still marvel at their beauty; one single stem in a vase, or bunches of flowers at the wholesale Flower Market at New Covent Garden. Their abundance, colour and fragrance can take one's breath away. Like sunshine itself, we are always pleased to see and be amongst flowers. Anyone studying or working with flowers should never be complacent; we are among the privileged to be involved with such beauty and variety.

Now, let us take a moment to consider our other word in the title: 'Imagination.' This is more difficult to pin down or describe. We cannot see or feel it, yet we know it exists. If the world would be a duller place without flowers, just imagine (that's the very word again) not having an imagination. I see it as a vital ingredient, the spring board from which our ideas can leap on to the stage and perform. We can become very 'airy fairy' using words like 'creativity' and 'magical' and this is fine, but as we conjure up a mass of ideas for our schemes and projects we must stay grounded.

Alan and I firmly believe in being organised. Ideas can flow like a river of possibilities in all creative work but the end result has to be workable. Structure, weight, balance, accessibility- all these aspects and many more have to be considered. As any flower designer or florist will know, water is the vital ingredient in nearly all work with flowers. So, I firmly believe that when imagination takes flight, as it must, we have to keep an eye continually on practicality. The two can go together hand in hand and very often the best work we see proves it.

To sum up this wonderful element in the human mind, we all need to use our imagination or we become becalmed, a sort of visual parallel to writer's block. So, go along with the tiniest speck of an idea. Invent, explore, experiment and it may well bloom and take stage in front of your very eyes. But do keep a weather eye open all the time on the specters of budget and cost; practicality waiting in the wings to halt your progress.

Our Imagination is a vital aspect of our daily lives. It can enhance our existence wherever we are in all circumstances. Use it, sit back and enjoy the amazing rewards it can bring.

A pretty bouquet in a teapot enhances any tea table.
Rosa (roses), Dianthus (carnation or pink), Eustoma (Lisianthus) and Senecio

A nest of paper encloses a single hydrangea.

The purest and most thoughtful minds
are those which love colour the most.

John Ruskin

Gillian loves creating bouquets, this particular one was created for H.R.H Princess Alexandra.
Rosa, Bouvardia, Hedera (ivy), Dianthus (carnation or pink), Agapanthus, Eupathorium

Amongst the dictionary definitions of bouquets we find "a cluster of flowers" and "a rosary", both of which I love for their simple description of the item. In its most basic form, a bouquet can be just a few simple flowers picked from the garden or hedgerow and tied together with a piece of string – the result, charming, and the recipient touched or delighted by the gift. On the other hand, we can create amazing hand-tied bunches in all sizes and combinations of colour and content.

My team are constantly creating bouquets for our customers. Some clients are very precise in their requests, knowing exactly the flowers and foliage they want, some are very vague or ask for the impossible. Then again, many choose a bouquet they like from our Academy range on our website. No two clients are alike and the fun part of the creating is in the putting together of different flowers to achieve something beautiful and attractive. All of our students at The Academy are taught how to create a hand-tied, as it is one of the most useful skills for the flower designer to master, especially for events such as a wedding, where the bouquet takes on a major role for the occasion.

Bouquets vary as I have said in both size and content and many of our bouquets are designed to be presented on stage at the end of a performance. Situated as we are in the heart of London's 'Theatre Land' much of our work is given to the performers of Ballet, Opera, Musicals and straight plays. The bouquets are designed to be seen in the spotlight and must have that 'wow' factor. I still get very excited to see our works on show in this manner.

The wonderful flip side of bouquets are their versatility. They can be placed in a container as they are, or used in any number of ways. Large bouquets containing a variety of flowers and foliage can be broken up and can easily create three or four separate arrangements in a number of containers. If kept in their own water bubble they can be strategically placed in the most unexpected situations. This can be seen in several of the images in this book.

A richly coloured background enhances this delicate bouquet.
Rosa, Muscari (grape hyacinth), Lavandula (lavender), Eustoma (Lisianthus)

Strong colours mingle with softer shades to add drama to this bouquet.
Rosa, Chamelaucium uncinatum (Geraldton wax flower), Quercus (oak), Brassica oleracea (ornamental cabbage)

Just roses for this wedding bouquet finished with tiny pearls that match the bride's gown.

A mirrored cube holds calla and roses.

A richly coloured autumn bouquet is placed in a pumpkin to reflect the shades of the season.
Rosa, Hedera (ivy), Skimmia, chillies, Zantedeschia (calla lily), Hypericum

The mixture of flowers, colours and textures chosen will always be unique.
Rosa, Zantedeschia (calla lily), Hypericum

I like to be inspired by the seasons and the colours they bring when creating a bouquet. Sometimes rich and bursting with a mass of blooms, sometimes pale and delicate using simple flowers and foliage to echo a theme.

The images that follow reflect this. A bouquet can convey the essence of any season or any idea you select.

The way we present our bouquets is very important too. Each florist or flower designer will have their preferences. Choice of tying materials varies too. It can be simple twine, cord raffia or a glamorous ribbon.

It can be wrapped in tissue or cellophane, or a combination of all of these factors right down to the card enclosed, or the bag, or the box that contains it. All of this will make the bouquet extra special.

A wired bouquet of Eustoma (Lisianthus).

A wired bouquet of Cymbidium, roses and Bouvardia.

A bouquet is placed in a ceramic boot.
Eustoma (Lisanthus), Hypericum, Chamelaucium uncinatum (Geraldton wax flower), Hydrangea.

Bouquets are very versatile. They can be placed in all manner of containers, large or small.

This one sits happily in a ceramic boot. The selection of a container for a posy or arrangement should be an important consideration when designing a piece.

Look for a variety of different styles and build up a collection over a period of time. This enables you to get maximum effect from your designs.

A hand tied summer bouquet in soft colours.
Rosa, Scabiosa, Eupatorium, Agapanthus, Salal.

Let's talk about the exciting subject of bouquets for a wedding. This is a very important event for any florist or flower designer. So many different areas have to be covered and because of the nature of the occasion, there are many opinions and voices to be listened to. Everyone has their own way of approaching this.

The old saying 'too many cooks spoil the broth', springs to mind, but I am a firm believer in listening closely to the bride, especially when designing her wedding bouquet and perhaps her bridesmaids' bouquets.

I see it as a personal decoration in harmony with the dress and ensemble. You cannot have too many discussions with a bride; it is after all going to be her day. Iron out any problems early and try to form a constructive and close working relationship with the bride. Naturally, one allows for the opinions and views of close family but I stress it is vital not to get side tracked, or water down a good idea to please a few people.

The bouquet you create for her on that special day is of prime importance. It will be filmed, photographed and be a constant reminder to the couple for years to come. Colour, texture and shape all play their part and when it works well, it completes the picture perfectly.

Rosa, Hedera (ivy)

Hydrangea, Rosa

This picture gives a new slant on presenting a bouquet.

The Agapanthus are tied and placed on an arrangement of glass shapes. The lighting enhances both form and colour.

Light direction and sources are very important and play a major part in the finished design. The light and the shadows it brings are always a vital factor in the placement of flowers in our home or at an event.

A gilt figure stands along side this purple posy on a period writing desk.
Rosa, Anenome (windflower)

Alan and I are often inspired by playing with a variety of flowers and other materials.

Hydrangea

Freshly gathered leaves and berries are tied together to form a very simple bunch.

The following image shows its placement in a specially made container. This was constructed from a wire bowl with grasses woven and attached.

The effect obtained was dramatic. This was used for a Christmas table.

Viburnum opulus, lily grass

Ranunculus are not only one of my favourite flowers, but we use them as a motif for our Academy. Here, they are simply tied and placed in a vase.

Celosia and elderflower gathered and tied give more of a contemporary look to this bouquet.
Celosia 'Olympia Series', Nicotiana, Sambucus (elderflower).

Genius is one per cent inspiration
and ninety-nine per cent perspiration.

Thomas Alva Edison

A simple posy of Hydrangeas on a cake stand.
Hydrangea

All white arrangement in a rose bowl.

Rosa, Bouvardia, Eustoma (Lisianthus), Eucalyptus pauciflora (snow gum), Lavandula (lavender) and Mimosa

Flowers, in all forms, are a staple in the work of the interior designer. I believe it is important to integrate your designs into the whole scheme in order to see the whole picture.

Sometimes flowers are dotted around an interior and although beautiful in themselves, they can end up looking like scattered confetti. There are no hard and fast rules and one designer's scheme may seem 'over the top', but when installed, looks fabulous.

There will always be focal points and you need to assess where these are from the start. As you enter the room or space take note of several aspects. Light (natural or artificial), will play a vital role in the finished effect. Another aspect is height, people in general do not look down or up naturally, so eye level becomes a very important area.

Mantelpieces, side tables, shelves etc. are always to be relied upon. It is wise to do a preliminary walk through and take note of all viewing aspects of the area.

This period mantelpiece holds an abundance of flowers for a wedding reception. The bride and groom expressed a desire to reflect all the fragrance and colour of an English garden.

Rosa, Eustoma (Lisianthus), Eucalyptus (gum tree), Hydrangea, Delphinium and Viburnum opulus

This flower scheme was specially commissioned by the Royal Ballet School in Richmond Park for the opening of the Darcy Bussel Studio.

The Gala dinner was held in the studio and was attended by H.R.H. the Prince of Wales and The Duchess of Cornwall.

The whole concept was to suggest lightness and movement. This is why I chose Phalaenopsis Orchids and Twisted Willow, as they lend a sense of gentle movement. Roses and soft blue Hydrangeas completed this romantic colour scheme.

Rosa, Hydrangea, Phalaenopsis, Schoenus melanostachys (flexi grass), Salix matsudana 'Tortuosa' (twisted willow)

This cascading arrangement on a mantelpiece makes a bold statement at the entrance for a wedding reception.

Paeonia, Rosa, Hydrangea, Eucalyptus (gum tree), Hedera (ivy)

Colour is always one of the designer's main areas of concern. What colours or patterns exist on walls or textiles will influence us greatly.

Our palette does not have to contrast or blend in. I feel that every situation is so different, that one cannot generalise.

Both Alan and I love to play with colour, line and form as we plan and install designs. Colour can make or break a design, and time spent selecting and matching is never wasted.

Fabrics, sea holly and fan coral are placed together in harmony. Textures and patterns, light and shade, form endless variations, as one plays and moves the items around. By playing with our raw materials, one can often discover a fresh aspect or a new way of using whatever is at hand. Sometimes even an accident or an unexpected clash will trigger a new approach to an idea.

Eryngium (sea holly)

Light, pattern and flowers all combine in this setting, each playing a vital part in the finished piece.
Agapanthus, Alchemilla mollis (lady's mantle)

I love putting patterns and flowers together. We often achieve unexpected results when the mix triggers off harmonies or clashes in colour and design.

Dappled sunlight can enhance any grouping of flowers and artefacts and will always add an extra element to our settings.

Flowers benefit immeasurably from placement near a light source, be it a lamp, wall fixture or daylight from a window. Surfaces sparkle with life, especially glass, lacquer, metal and ceramics. Grouping, as with the flowers themselves, is a very important factor and well worth the effort.

Your flowers can be placed against bold stripes, checks or floral designs, which will fight with your designs to dominate. I love mixing patterns as in a patchwork, but where flowers and foliage are concerned, I am wary. What may look wonderful and dynamic in a magazine spread may not be easy to live with.

In general, plain or textured backgrounds will show off your designs to good effect. If strong patterns are unavoidable, design accordingly.

Here the arrangement in the vase was designed especially to echo the seasonal mood of the wallpaper behind it.

Quercus (oak), Salix caprea (pussy willow), Salix matsudana 'Tortuosa' (twisted willow), Calla and Crocosmia (Montbretia)

Here is another example of coordinating flowers with backgrounds. The Ilex berries and redwood are real and appear to spring from the realistic printed wall paper.
Cornus (dogwood), Ilex (holly)

Yellow roses sit happily against a soft muted background. Ceramics and bronze make for a mellow mood that sets off the colour to perfection.

Hydrangea, grape stalks

The surprise element, as I have stated elsewhere, is a trump card that the designer can play frequently. Interiors offer us the perfect setting for unusual placements and ideas. They do not always have to be practical or down to earth.

Flowers can appear in all manner of places and settings and do not always have to be in water. I have, on occasions, had flowers hanging upside down, perched on the shoulder of a statue or bust, or laid out in patterns on tables like mosaics. Think outside the box sometimes, amuse the onlooker and gladden the eye.

Search out an unexpected situation for a posy or a bouquet, they may only need to last for a few hours but the impact and comments they arouse will be remembered.

Pink calla lilies placed on the figures shoulder, add colour and interest.

Roses add a theatrical touch to this dramatic bust.
Rosa, Hedera (ivy)

Alan is always on the look out for materials
not normally associated with flowers.
In this design he has used a tubular bandage
and pulled it over a plain glass vase.

With this method endless variations can
be experimented with. The bandage has
a neutral colour and a pleasing texture but
it could be dyed or painted in any colour.

By placing the design against architectural
prints the effect is harmonious.

The golden bird is set off by scarlet velvet and spheres made up from star anise and hazelnuts. This made a rich and glowing Christmas table decoration.

These two spheres made from nuts make for a decorative feature.

Pink calla lilies brighten this group in a study. The ball is covered in dried Magnolia leaves and takes on the look of polished leather.

Dried Allium heads are here set against driftwood.
Their spider like shapes contrast well with the rugged wood.

I am always on the lookout for objects and figures that will blend into interesting groupings.

The Pierrot figure is a case in point. The arrangement of red roses picks up the romantic mood and adds warmth to the setting.

Rosa, Eucalyptus

For a private party at the London Ritz we designed one arrangement that ran the length of the table.
Rosa, Eustoma (Lisianthus), Alchemilla mollis, Eucalyptus.

Events play a very important role in the world of flower design. They can be impressive with hundreds of guests, or small and intimate for a special, private occasion. It is impossible to categorize them in this media driven age as they vary so much. As with weddings, the client's briefing session is a vital part of the planning strategy. Once again, themes and ideas drive the event along.

The artistic realisation of the design at the exhibit or event is what the public will see, so it is essential that the chosen theme is the right one. All the unseen elements – the logistics, the time management, the costing, the buying and the installation will all be as important and cannot be overlooked at any stage.

I always take a great deal of time when planning an event for a client. Mainly to ensure that they will be delighted with the resulting scheme, colours, visual impact and such like. Even more important is the reaction of the guests who will see the work first hand. It is this feedback from our designs being on view that matters, the response is all important. We can score on all levels and build our reputation aesthetically and commercially. It is good practice to keep records of all events undertaken for future reference. A later viewing with colleagues or clients can trigger suggestions to adapt or improve.

Rows of black containers were filled with Ilex and redwood topped with moss. These were designed for a television gala. At The Academy, we liken the versatility of these little black boxes to the ever useful little black dress, as shown in the following photographs.

Conus (dogwood), Ilex (holly), Moss

A bold, dramatic colour scheme was used for the launch of a new Jaguar model.

The black bowls appear this time in repetition, running the whole length of the table.

The reflective surfaces play a major role in the finished design.

Celosia and Agapanthus africanus (African lily)

The red Celosia and the blue Agapanthus contrast with the black shining glass cubes.

Close up of Celosia and roses.

Black cubes give way to black bowls, again the repetition emphasises their form and surface.

Rosa and Agapanthus africanus (African lily)

Red parrot tulips in black cubes at Goldsmiths Hall London were used for a presentation of work in precious metals.

Corporate events, parties and celebrations of all types, large or small, play a major role in the day to day working life of the flower designer. They happen throughout the year and the event team is always kept busy with the planning and finishing of installations.

We work closely with the clients brief and take great trouble to ensure that everything comes together on the day, with the caterers, entertainment and the lighting technicians- all of this is essential. Due to the fragile nature of our creations, how the arrangements are transported and placed in the venue is always a top priority.

The 'get in and out' stages of many events has to run like clockwork, as so many people are involved. When it all comes together the effects can be magical, very similar to a first night at the theatre but as the events are usually for one night only, there is no room for error.

Very tall, oversized Champagne flutes were used to give height and impact in this venue. This was for a private corporate event in London.
Eucalyptus pauciflora (snow gum sprayed gold), Rosa, Hedera (ivy), Salix matsudana 'Tortuosa' (twisted willow), Antirrhinum (snapdragon), Ornithogalum (Chincherinchee)

This ornate mirror has been decorated to echo the surrounding décor.
This was for a private Christmas celebration.
Eucalyptus pauciflora (snow gum sprayed gold), Laurus (lavender sprayed white), Zantedeschia aethiopica 'Green Goddess' (calla lily)

A close up of the table arrangement seen on a previous page.

These were created in a basement underneath the venue. They were then transported up three flights of stairs.

It was a nerve racking experience for all. We repeated this for forty table centres.

A glamorous function in Mayfair for over four hundred guests used colour as its main attraction. The colours and theatrical lighting played a very important part on this occasion.

The Academy was asked to create table settings for a gala evening at the Coliseum for the English National Opera.

A ship in a bottle with driftwood depicts The Flying Dutchman.

Eustoma (Lisianthus), Gypsophila, Limonium (Statice), Agapanthus africanus (African lily)

This arrangement was for a Gala evening for the English National Opera at the Banqueting House in Whitehall.
Salix matsudana 'Tortuosa' (twisted willow), Hedera (ivy), Rosa, Agapanthus africanus (African lily), Eustoma (Lisianthus), (Singapore orchid) and Schoenus melanostachys (flexi grass)

This arrangement for the English National Opera depicts The Magic Flute.
Rosa, Hedera (ivy), Eustoma (Lisianthus), Chamelaucium uncinatum (Geraldton waxflower), Agapanthus africanus (African lily)

Alan and I were having fun in our studio with driftwood, Magnolia leaves and Agapanthus.

We both enjoy using the circular form.

This candle arrangement in the hurricane lamp is one we use frequently.

Not only is it attractive but very safe which is a major consideration at events. It also adapts well to all seasons.

Rosa, Hedera (ivy), Brassica oleracea (ornamental cabbage), Quercus (oak) and waxed apples

On occasions, arrangements in the home can take the shape of a still life grouping. This form of putting objects and flowers together has been popular with artists, stylists and designers for many years.

Items such as nests, driftwood, boxes, fruits and such like can all be brought into play to make interesting and attractive set pieces. I like to reflect the mood and colour of an art work with flowers and foliage sometimes merging the two seamlessly.

Students enjoy going to one of the London galleries, choosing a picture to interpret in the studio with flowers and foliage. The resulting creations always cause much discussion and comment.

Eucalyptus pauciflora (snow gum), Hedera (ivy), Rosa, grapes and Asparagus

Bleached wood and Alliums make for a dramatic composition. The effect is heightened by the lighting which throws strong shadows.

What the imagination seizes as beauty must be truth, whether it existed before or not.

John Keats

Gardens, terraces and patios are wonderful areas to place our creations. Everyone expects to see flowers and plants in borders, beds or containers, so it is always something of a surprise to discover the unexpected.

Dining alfresco is forever a pleasure and flowers can play their part as table decorations, but try something a little different. Alan and I have tried out many schemes for friends and clients, among them covering an entire table with a cloth of autumn leaves pressed and lightly glued to soft muslin.

For evenings outside we often just place freshly picked flowers: Roses, Hydrangeas, Daises and the like, alongside large swathes of leaves like Fatsia and Eucalyptus – the effect will be stunning.

These creations will stay fresh for hours and there is no need for water.

A hand tied creation of calla lilies and Agapanthus sit on top of an ornate fountain.
Zantedeschia (calla lily) and Agapanthus

The garden or terrace is a perfect place to surprise guests.

Posies or small bouquets of flowers can be placed on figures or garden furniture.

Benches, ledges or niches make the perfect setting for your creations.

Still life with Alliums in a shady corner of the garden.

On occasion, Alan has covered small side tables by laying a pattern of leaves in all shades and textures. It makes a natural sort of mosaic and can be dismantled in minutes. Other materials can be incorporated for unusual effects. Cleverly placed mirrors with their reflections double the impact of your design and never fail to be a talking point for guests. Take a good look at those areas where the house meets the garden - there is plenty of potential.

A stone cherub holds a cornucopia topped with a cluster of Hydrangea and Rosa.

Fatsia, Hosta (plantain lily), Geranium (cranesbill)

Zantedeschia (calla lily), Agapanthus

A circular mirror strategically placed in a hedge reflects an arrangement of Alliums.

Rosa, Zantedeschia (calla lily), Hedera (ivy), Alchemilla mollis (lady's mantle), Fatsia, Hydrangea

Rosa, Hydrangea

Rosa, Zantedeschia (calla lily), Hedera (ivy), Alchemilla mollis (lady's mantle), Fatsia, Hydrangea

Dawn Dusk
By Alan Wheeler

These are my favourite times in the garden.
The dawn chorus is over, clouds are lifting to reveal a watery sun.
The soft night rain has refreshed us all, and the leaves
are left as if embroidered with tiny crystal-like droplets.

The grass moist and green holds footprints as I cross the lawn.
It will be a good day. The sun now setting on the horizon
sends its last rays to paint the white roses amber gold.
Lights and murmuring voices come from the house.

I finish my glass of cool white wine. I have been sitting under
the apple tree, a tree as old as the house itself.

I bolt the doors and turn to look once more at the garden
ready for more night rain as it sinks into shadows.

Alchemilla mollis (lady's mantle)

Flowers make a decorative addition to this orrery.

Balls made from chrysanthemums look like peas in a pod within this shape, making an eye catching feature in the garden.
Chrysanthemum

The balcony at The Royal Ballet School in Richmond Park is festooned with flowers and foliage for an event.
Rosa, Hedera (ivy), Lonicera (honeysuckle), Anthriscus Sylverstris (cow parsley)

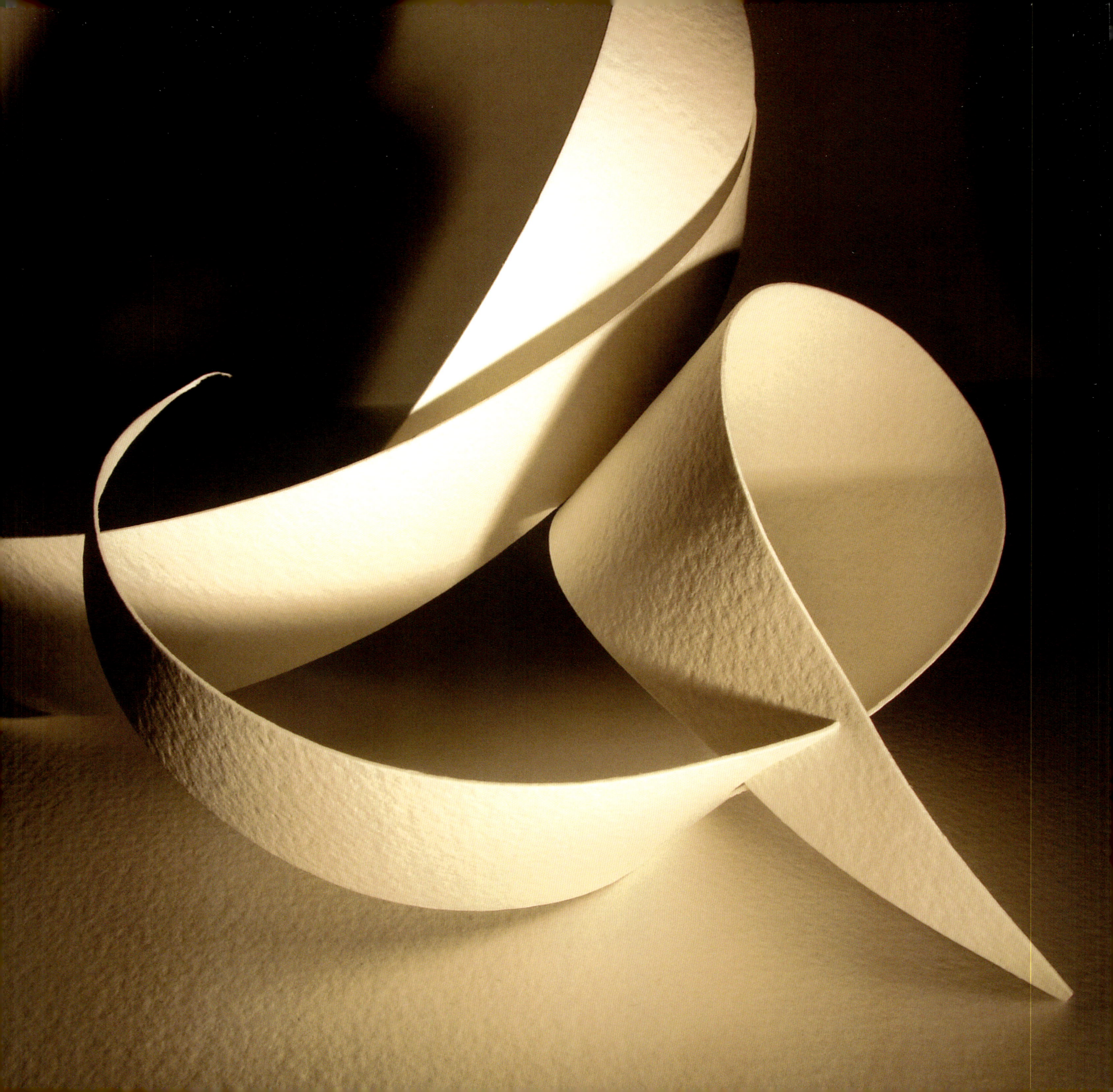

History has remembered the kings and warriors, because they destroyed; art has remembered the people, because they created.

William Morris

Paper and its long history make a fascinating subject for study, but within the context of our book I want us to see how we can combine it with flowers and foliage.

As this is Alan's great passion along with all manner of other materials, I pass you over to his expertise on all matters involving craft skills in presentation and styling.

Whilst, like Gillian, I have always loved flowers and foliage, my display/styling background has led me into experimenting with a wide range of other materials.

Gillian never fails to be surprised to find me involved in cutting, gluing, shredding and dying all manner of things. It is by playing with, and using such materials that we discover hidden or unexpected techniques.

Zantedeschia (calla lily)

This fragile bowl was created by Gillian for a photo shoot.
It is made from skeletonised leaves and pressed ferns.
Note the change of mood between natural sunlight and studio lighting.

In my years with Liberty's display team, I specialised in handling and draping beautiful fabrics.

Years later, whilst teaching the subject of display, I found myself drawn to creating with paper.

I found it to be a fascinating material to work with, as it can vary so much in weight and texture, from tissue-like, Japanese papers to heavy art papers, which can be sculpted into amazing forms.

Zantedeschia (calla lily)

At The Academy, Gillian loves to encourage students to bring other elements into their work.

I visit regularly and try to stimulate creativity by demonstrating the combination of flowers and other materials.

These can be incorporated into backgrounds, on containers or just as an addition to a finished piece.

Gillian has placed this small china doll against an amusing picture of toys. Pink Roses and Hellebores in a vase complete the grouping.

All papers and fabrics need handling and
it is how they are manipulated that transforms
a sheet of paper or a length of taffeta.

As in couture, the design and cutting makes
for a stunning result or a disaster.

Practice is the key and familiarity with
whatever it is you have chosen to work
with will always pay dividends.

Hydrangea, Acer (maple)

An antiqued collage background sets off this wired corsage.
Rosa, Hyacinthus (hyacinth), Chamelaucium (Geraldton waxflower), Hypericum, Hedera (ivy)

Contrasts between the text, background and
the sculptured feather are dramatised by spotlighting.

I love working with all manner of materials from wire mesh to felt, net, plaster. Bleaching, shredding, assembling, dismantling are all part of my studio day.

After doing this for many years one would assume the brain would tire but I can truthfully say I still get that same buzz when approaching a new sheet of paper or a roll of fabric - they present me with all manner of challenges.

This image is a perfect example of what I aim for. The heavy Arches paper had to be soaked in the bath before manipulating it into a striking form.

Phyllostachys (bamboo), Sambucus (elderflower), grape stalks, Hydrangea

I often create hats from heavy watercolour paper for the Academy window displays.

I always try to include a flower or two, real or artificial, they always attract comments from students and customers.

These costumes were created for two Royal Ballet School students.
Each piece was wired separately.

144

This hat was created by Madeleine, one of The Academy team using real flowers and foliage.

Silver metal mesh merges with white Agapanthus.
The effect is light and free.

This large picture hat in white
was featured in a wedding promotion.
Paeonia (peony), Rosa, Nigella, Stephanotis

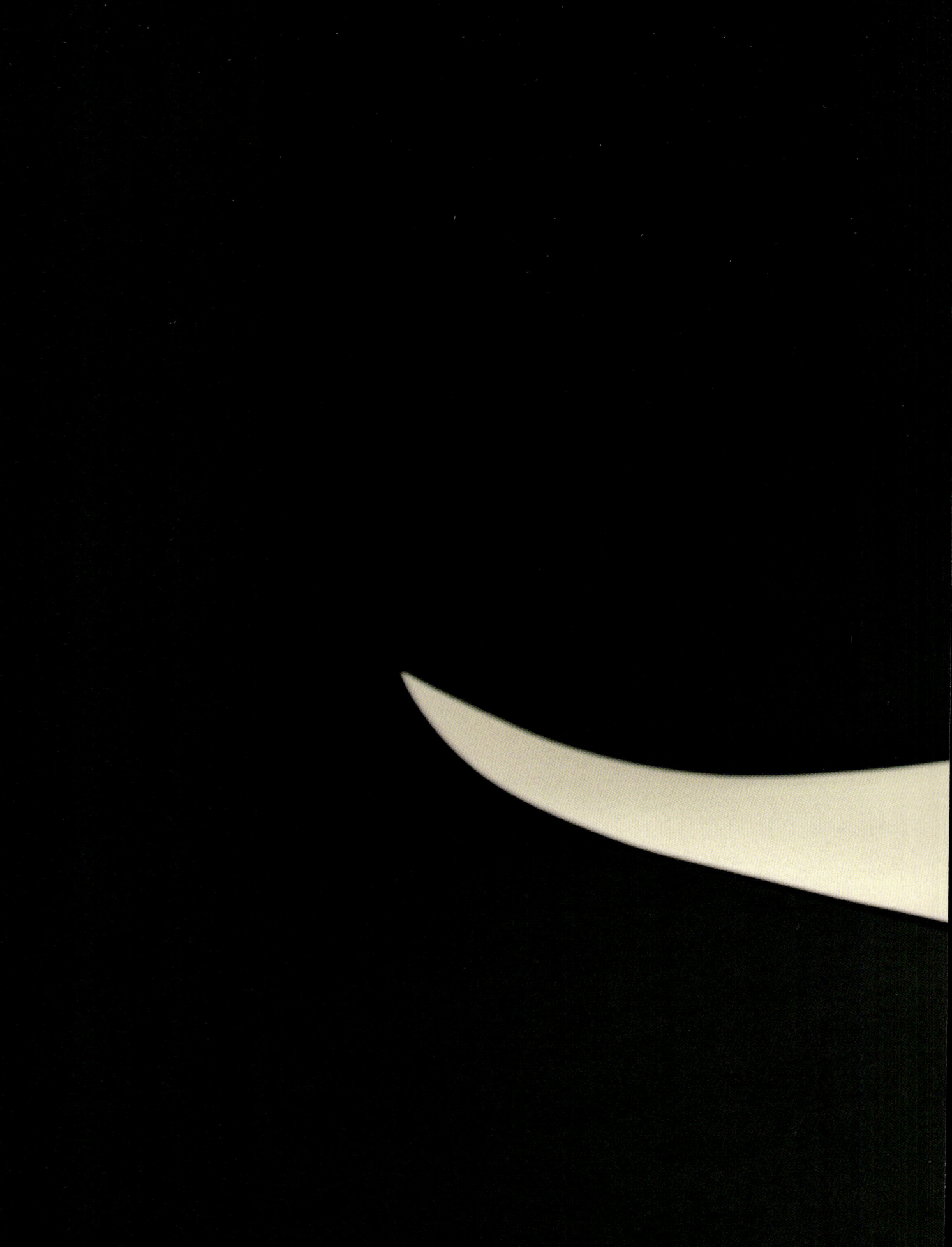

The Covent Garden Academy of Flowers is bringing the colour and magic of flowers back to Covent Garden.

Covent Garden is known all over the world as a place that offers an abundance of experiences, brought to life for millions through the film 'My Fair Lady'- the story of Covent Garden flower-seller, Eliza Dolittle. The area breathes creativity for artists, designers and performers. It is a breeding ground for new ideas.

The Academy's courses provide students with all the elements needed to bring their imagination to centre stage. Students learn all the tricks and skills of the florist, but above and beyond that they seize upon the potential for real design.

The Academy provides a range of facilities, studio spaces, presentation and preparation areas, flower chill rooms, work-shops, library and study areas and a full range of support facilities. The Academy Store has a wide range of Academy merchandise and a regular array of seasonal flowers and floral offers.

The Academy has become one of Covent Garden's must see locations.

The Duchess of Cornwall during an official visit to the Covent Garden Academy of Flowers.

Biography

Gillian Wheeler

Gillian Wheeler is the founder and Principal of The Covent Garden Academy of Flowers. Gillian has had an interesting career in graphic design, presentation and visualisation, involving a variety of exhibition work, and has taught Flower Design for over twenty years. Gillian has an MA in Design Studies from Central St Martins. She has always had a passion for flowers, which has enabled her to fuse her training in design and her love of flowers into the successful flower design courses that she managed at the University of the Arts London for over fifteen years. Gillian has worked on a variety of projects for many high profile clients and venues such as Kew Gardens, The English National Opera, Tate Modern, The Saatchi Gallery, Natural History Museum, The Royal Ballet and the Queen for her Diamond Jubilee in 2012.

Alan Wheeler

Alan has had a long and varied career in the fields of display and staging. An author of two books on the subject, he has experienced all aspects of styling and presentation. His seven years as a member of the display team at Liberty's gave him a wide range of experience, enabling him to move in to lecturing and demonstrating. As a course director at The University of the Arts London he spanned over thirty years training students in all aspects of art and display. Add to this a wealth of commissions and seminars for such clients as the V&A, Kew Gardens, The Royal Horticultural Society, Constance Spry, NAFAS, Asprey and Arjo Wiggins. His love of paper and textiles still keeps him busy at The Academy where he is a frequent visiting tutor.

Thank you

Alan and I would like to thank many people
who contributed to this book.

For the concept and title we owe our gratitude
to Jaak Van Damme our publisher
– without his inspiration and advice the book
would never have materialised.
Add to Jaak all his team at Stichting Kunstboek
for their expertise and dedication.

For our daughter Fleur whose help has been
inspirational and invaluable.

Albert Fielder for his creative advice and input.

Richard Webb for the forword to this book.

The Academy team for their support and help.

Students of the Academy
for constantly being there when needed.

Thank you to the Royal Ballet School students
for wearing our floral costumes

Most of the images in the book were created
and photographed by Gillian herself
with the exceptions listed below.
All paper images were created by Alan.

Guy Hearn pages 29, 30
Jeff Carrigan pages 32, 33, 36, 37, 39, 65, 139, 154
Alex Brenner page 86
Mark Livermore pages 80, 81, 84, 85, 142, 143, 153
Madeleine Mukherjee for the creation on page 144

Colophon

Author
Gillian and Alan Wheeler

The Covent Garden Academy of Flowers
St Martin's Courtyard 9
Slingsby Place
Covent Garden
WC2E 9AB London
United Kingdom
Tel. +49 20 7240 6359
www.academyofflowers.com

Photography
The Covent Garden Academy of Flowers

Lay-out
Group Van Damme
www.groupvandamme.eu

Print
PurePrint
www.pureprint.be

Published by
Stichting Kunstboek bvba
Legeweg 165
B-8020 Oostkamp
Belgium
Tel. +32 50 46 19 10
Fax + 32 50 46 19 18
info@stichtingkunstboek.com
www.stichtingkunstboek.com

ISBN 978-90-5856-433-7
D/2013/6407/23
NUR 421

The authors and publisher have made every effort to find and correctly attribute the copyright of material that is not already in the public domain but if they have inadvertently used or credited any material inappropriately, please could the copyright holder contact the authors or publisher so that a full credit can be given in the next edition.

All rights reserved. No part of this book may be reproduced, stored in a database or a retrieval system, or transmitted in any form or by any means, electronically, mechanically, by print, microfilm or otherwise without prior permission in writing from the publisher.

© Stichting Kunstboek 2013